SMELTER

poetry
from theTees Valley
2003

selected by
Cynthia Fuller and Kevin Cadwallender

Publishing the Fog

Mudfog Press was formed ten years ago. Since 1993 we have been committed to publishing the best new writing from Teesside. We have now published 43 pamphlets of poetry and short-stories, as well as 9 full-length books. This collection is our tenth.

During the last ten years many key institutions of the local literary scene have folded - notably the Leeds University Adult Education Centre in Middlesbrough, the annual Writearound festival, literature development in Cleveland Arts, Buzzwords, the *Evening Gazette* 'Write On' page, Cleveland LEA, the Urdu-English *musha'ara* and Poetry Live! The future is less clear. Will the Tees Valley Cultural Strategy be more than words in the wind? Will Arts Council NE put in new support and resources? Will the five unitary authorities – now Darlington is officially in there – be able to link their initiatives and aspirations for the support, promotion and success of literature? Will higher education find a role in nurturing local writing? Will local writers have the determination to win audiences and wider success?(1)

Meanwhile, Mudfog's regional and national reputation as the publisher of good books has continued to grow. One of our titles was chosen as Book of the Month in *Just 17* ; another is currently being adapted for the theatre. Several Mudfog authors have since gone on to be published elsewhere. Mudfog has helped to put a part of Britain often dismissed as a cultural desert on the literary map. (2)

Smelter is a measure of how far poets from our area and poetry about this area have developed during the last decade. There are some 80 poems here from 34 poets, whose differences are often striking. Since Mark Robinson's *A Hole Like That* (Scratch appeared in 1994, the variety his collection celebrated has expanded further. 34 poets from 13. Women now in the majority. Teesside/Tees Valley identity spreading its wings out to life in Tyneside and Normandy.

These poems have come into existence in a kind of Virtual Teesside of the imagination, a place with long and complex histories and legends, with short and uncertain futures. There are strengthening signals here from a distinctive voice. Unapologetic. realistic. Knowing where it comes from, having some love for that ready to move on. A touch of resignation. More than a whiff of defiance, as if to say, " Who are you looking at?" We all need to work on that voice, as it asks questions about identity, history, difference, place and belonging. *Smelter* aims to fuse those many questions to weigh up our place in the world out there - how does it look from the banks of the Tees and how do we look from out there?

The imagination is also where we will begin to create and explore the new myths of Tees Valley, a place of strategies and government-funded optimism. Political, cultural, economic, sociological and imaginative borders shift and change; poets need to be alert to where their poetry lives. Perhaps the 2013 Mudfog anthology will reflect all that. Perhaps it will also reflect shifting patterns of cultural identity, as higher education and global crises bring into this river/sea settlement writers with different experiences, varied languages, unexpected perceptions, new poetries. We look forward to publishing them all.

Editorial Board, Mudfog Press

(1) See Andy Croft, 'Magic, Mimesis and Middlesbrough' in Mark Robinson (ed) *Words Out Loud*, (Stride, 2000)
(2) See Andy Croft, 'Fire and Horror : the Representation of Teesside in Fiction' in Gustav Klaus and Steven Knight (eds) *Industrial Fictions* (University of Wales Press, Cardiff, 2000)

Selecting the Fog

In the first read through you look for individual poems that stand out from the rest. There will be something that grabs your attention - a freshness of language, a surprising use of imagery, something exciting about the form. You are aware of accumulating single poems that have a 'buzz' about them. Sharing the editing makes the process much more interesting. Seeing where you differ, being prepared to re-assess and to have another look at poems that you've overlooked makes you clarify your own criteria. We agreed on a high proportion of our choices, and where there were differences they were often about choosing between particular poems by the same poet. This made the process a very smooth one.

The strangest part of the process is the way in which the selected individual poems take on a group identity. The poets' brief produced some recurring subjects - Teesside past and present, urban and rural landscapes, and the detail of everyday lives. But the themes are wide and the poems engage with the specific as well as the universal. Poems contemplate the world with nostalgia, with anger, with sharp satirical wit. The voices are distinct; the poems demonstrate a range of technique and form and an awareness of an imposing tradition of writing in the Teesside area. However they are universal as well as regional expanding beyond their own boundaries, both geographically and emotionally.

The core of writing in Teesside is distinct and strong, flavoured with wry honesty and tempered by the urban industrial landscape it finds itself in; tipping over into the outlying areas of rural and semi-rural, warm and tough, frank and charming. A smelter of words.

Cynthia Fuller and Kevin Cadwallender
Mudfog's Guest Selectors

Note: Poets were invited to submit up to six poems for this collection. Our Guest Selectors were asked to make their selection from all the work submitted.

Smelter - The Line Up

Author	Title or first line	Page

Curlew

Some dig,
some watch the surface
for the slightest trace of movement.
No one sits on the fence.

In fields beyond the flats, males gather,
wait for the moon to move the water;
for the slow tide
to hand things on a plate.

At Teesmouth,
on these Seal Sands,
size does matter;
long female beaks
burrow into breathing mud,
catch the fattest lugs.

Maureen Almond

Greetings from the far North

where I have been sweeping
the yard of leaves, snail shells and earth
shivering in the morning ice
the gold eye of a fish under frozen water

you glide about the capital
in leather and silk
multiplying your assets
now I have been subtracted

here the wind plucks a drone
across the fields a sea of jade frost
the sky a wash of plum blossom

people's mushroom faces
above the collars like moist compost

the children scream and whirl
like seagulls starved by storms at sea

if you come back
you will come back hungry
defensive as a right angle
watching me add coal to the fire.

Pauline Plummer

Cogida

Up here on Murder Hill the earth is losing
control of its store of August heat which lifts
and breaks towards the persistent tug of a rising
harvest moon. You scoff at twelve-hour shifts:
tonight, with a bullfighter's concentration, you guide
sharp fingers across the field below and peel
up laid corn; indifferent to what's on either side;
aware of nothing but barley cowled to your reel.
If an auger stalls or a drive belt slips
you'll pause, back up to free some trash, draw
one hand up over your brow and moisten your lips –
that's all. You heard about the matador
who stole a glance at a woman in the crowd.
None of it's true, I tell you. Look up now.

Katharine Banne

Cogida is the term used for the tossing of a bullfighter by a bull.
The literal translation from Spanish is a *gathering of the harvest*.

Introductions with French pupils

Madame

      Yes

Where do you come from?

      Middlesbrough

Middle what?
It's in the middle of where (no where?)
Brough not borough

But why?

Middlesbrough Football Club!

      Well, yes … how do you know?

Caramburgh played for them

      Really? How interesting …
      Now what about Captain Cook?

Capitaine who?

      Cook

Tunafish

      Sorry?

Grandname

      Bizarre
      Now repeat after me, Middlesbrough

Meadlesbrew!?!?

Ghazala Bashir

Shaun and Darren go shopping

They're meant to be at school learning important stuff.
The lifecycle of the lemon scented geranium, the French words
        for trousers,
how to divide odd numbers quickly and easily.
The meaning of life.

But personal development and social skills have passed these
        boys by.
They've developed as far as humanly possible,
given the fact that they can't see the point sir.
Social skills are wasted on the young, and they spent the
        dinner/sinner money hours ago.

Shaun and Darren have a shopping list of necessities.
CDs, sportswear, computer games.
They are invincible, ride the crowds like surfers,
unerring and strong in their white tracksuit bottoms
and brand new nicked Nike trainers.

Carol Cook

Running

the gauntlet of the roman road past the college
disturbing a box-terrier sniffing a dropped slice of pizza
in a squashed Manhattan box, still displaying the skyline
just as it was, head afloat in absinth & a traveller's tales
of Haiti stripping down the deceits of interest free Bohemia;
with poverty like he'd never seen, war-talk & the day
of reckoning looming over a bed warmed by love
in the Little Houses by the Water snoring stars out bright
no moon nor wind nor snow but the always orange haze
of streetlights swilling half-way up the basin, fireworks
finally fading, festive lights twinkling & the pretty pink neons
aglow on Centre North East like Jacob's Ladder got him
mulling over Bernicia & all the feudal lines drawn up
between the Tees & the Tyne, the Wear & the Tweed
the Prince Bishopdom, the Dane-law, De Brus' estates
the precious shifts in vowel sounds, inherited battlegrounds
sweet Lucia de Thweng in a secret castle out by Skelton
the maccam's yards & all those mines of ransacked ore;
then foot-stumbling as if caught on the chin by a image
of St Hilda first facing the Headland with a stiff upper lip
or King Oswy cuffing him while considering the potential
lineage of kingship & at the cemetery gates he was hailed
by a Mohawk brave and a tribe of stillborn babes
recently remembered in stone, saw the Quakers of Port Darlo'
moving themselves into new plots overnight &
was reminded momentarily of Bosnia Herzegovina
the warring maps of mis-matched histories; a sharp flash
of film footage of a man running naked from a bomb-shelled
arm full of family corpses & Daniel from the corner
his Mam & Dad trying asylum in the Boro & unavoidably
thought up the mind-bite of two crumbling towers:
capitalism & a New World Order Ever Falling Thoughts
about how it felt this past year for those who kept
an ear close to the ground like things were happening here
like this town was going places: Paris Milan Ground Zero

Sarajevo Baghdad The Great Land of Leather PC World
wherever whenever & for how long no one can say
because it's never what you expect it to be this town's
not what you project it to be then he's thinking of
The Faraway Tree & it seems a suitable analogy
for a town off the cuff - too used to making itself up
to reply to the rhetoric of *so whoo dooya wannabe*
with anything more than a cynical shrug (*inshallah*)
with the river turning tricks across the width of the basin
changing course & claiming old debts like Jack's Victoria
Cross the pocket Bible of an unknown soldier souvenir
postcards from Cork a shotgun in a sportsbag a book
of love poems from Pakistan, pouring the Good & the Bad
of it between unflinching Gares into breakers struggling
to believe in the past of a future geography we might
peg a hope on this New Year's Eve that despite & because
of it all's as soft and shiny as a park mallard's wing.

Bob Beagrie

Abstract

Large white frame
Full square concrete
grey on grey. Artex
surface snags nylons
like grit in a dead oyster. Flashes
of heliotrope, acid yellow   clash
across slashing black
red/white/red/white stripes
No harmony of texture, colour, shape

Steel clasp purse sealed tight
Newport Bridge screwed shut
Transporter broken down again
- warring acute angles point
stab at the sick river, going nowhere
sticks, needles, index fingers
jab at my soft belly

                                       Central hammer drill
                       tries
          to dominate my eye
        fails
as I am drawn
        towards the edge
            over the border

                  In the corner
                      black dog cringes
                            worries the dove

                            Marilyn Longstaff

The Works

Derelict, the rusting rails,
broken fences,
overgrown embankments,
litter and graffiti.
Once alive with workers,
illuminated generously
to dispel the gloom.
The works shrugged off
hard times and setbacks,
but today the accountants have won.
Each man's life
a mere tick on a tally,
calculated profit and loss,
another piece to move
in the Monopoly game.
Go to the dole,
move directly to the dole,
do not pass go,
do not collect £200.
You must throw less than 45
to get another job.

Brian Morton

The Hills Are Far Too Big To Eat

The hills are far too big to eat
but they make me so hungry
and the cheeks and backs of them
look like they'll just fit me

so I went up them today
but there was nothing at all.
No grip for your shoes and no shapes.
No noises, just thick, wet air

till a great gold shaft cleft right through
from the sun to the steelworks
sandcastling it at the seaside
fantastic, gorgeous

then it clouded over again.
When I was down, going home
on the plain, it was all fields
and the hills stood round like a crown.

Liz Geraghty

Huntcliff

Across the valley from the ordered town
My eyes follow a skyline sweeping down
The contours of patched and folded fields
Right up to Huntcliff's brutal edge.

It stands   a slab   a great red wedge
                a giant stepping off of land
down to where a lazy pillowed sea
rolls unhurriedly to shore
                so light its touch   it hardly
moves the shell and shingle flotsam
with its swell

and in the middle air between   sea birds
yelp and scream   stammer out a wild
music   every ledge and foothold
        veined with gulls / the air   snow-thick with gulls
        circling stiff on wind-thrummed wings
drifting   veering and rearing against
the updraught   stall   free-fall
                slide aslant the wall of wind
then out and away where toy boats queue up in the bay

another day / a month or million years before
        or since   who can say
for only seasons matter not the years
                the great cliff stands vacant
                and in the evening / by a trick of light
        at the water's highest reach   it's an
abandoned tanker let run deep into the beach
        in this natural breaker's yard battering waves drum
a hard tattoo on ribs and keel   on underpinnings
        jack-hammering winds play rat-a-tat
on the top-most riggings   prising   pulling
peeling away   and no boats ride at anchor in the bay.

Geoff Strang

Tour Guide

Bluster down Corporation,
Left at the lights, amber, green, who cares?
Time enough to whirl around Victoria
Visit the library, dodge the courts
And dry the pigeon shit on old Mr Bolckow.

Straight over to Grange, round
The round unlidded eyes that
See me buffet Big Macs
Scatter and sow chips and shakes.

Blast along Linthorpe dragging
Diesel fumes and pizza smells
Slamming doors and swinging signs.

Divide and conquer at the Crescent
Heading buses and taxis off at the pass.

Right turn on Roman, billowing
On to Burlam, whispering through
Yews and Oaks that shade the silent residents.

Swirling into Whinney Banks, sieving
Through the mesh of empty homes.

Spiralling out over Newport, chilling the evening rush.
Beading the nipples at Cannon Park,
Blueing the knees at Union,
Chasing those dragons that coil on the air;
Circling, searching, whistling and howling
For ways to blow this town.

Gary Ming

Earthwired

Skirt trailing in baked earth, running cracks
big enough to lose a rabbit down.
The wind dies. On this hill top.

North: of Freeborough Hill,
where an ancient prince lies dreaming.
South: of the North Sea,
where Skinningrove Beck veins into the surf.
East: of a shale pyramid,
where scarab beetles scuttle slag.
West: of Liverton Mine terraces
where women with telescopes hide behind net curtains.
Skyward: of Kilton Valley
Where lost Normans track the wood trails still.

On this hill top, the wind dies.
Rabbits are lost down holes, running
like cracks in baked earth. Trailing my skirt,

I listen for:
the wind ruffling the hairs on a bluebottle's legs;
the soft shuuush of a swift, circling an ox-eye daisy
like a hawk;
the scurrying of woodlice under rotting logs;
the creaking of the earth, settling into graves;
the butterfly fluttering in Liverton wombs
once thought of as mined out.

On this hill top;
in baked earth, trailing a skirt
big enough to lose rabbits in; down holes
running like cracks, the wind dies.

Val Mage

Sunday Morning, Reading Drabble

who mentions a gnarled hand
with its embedded ring.
At least I haven't yet
got my hands gnarled,
the ring is loose enough
just wedged below the joint.
Troubled, I still look down -
not quite gnarled, though gnarling
f clock's hands can gnarl.
Or is it 'being gnarled'
as trees that ring our years
all in this October
all their leaves out there
where next door's building
a conservatory, the sun's new trap
on shared south-facing wall?

f we tried to spring such a snap
on godhead, snaky-haired,
so feared and revelled in?
Divinity that sets bait for us all
ets us build our cages, has us
write *if he is willing* in inky flame
on every policy we're sold.
That has given us fire,
watches us torch our own,
roast the whole street indeed.
That watches anything but:
each tedious outrage under heaven
led as a claim on deficit interest.

Sunday, early trees and silence.
The sun slips into winter,
ght-fingers through the pages
s secularity, touches such questions
s are here in morning
where distant author plays
with gnarling reader, takes this day
f not-for-long autumnal brightness
t its best, does not quite find faith
n inconclusive loveliness,
he life short and almost unbearable.

Gordon Hodgeon

War and rumours of War

Even in winter this mid-town cherry
tree is full of life. Catching morning sun
over Middleton Terrace followed by
afternoon warmth over the scrap yard
the other side of the railway. Its bare
branches a resting place for feathered
messengers refused entry to the ark.
No place to tell their tales, give their warnings.

Bluetits clean round fattening buds keeping
insect enemies at bay, whilst further
east guns are cleaned preparing for war.

Redstarts rest here on their journey elsewhere
flashing red for danger as they take to flight.
Blackbirds and thrushes stop by to take stock
before chittering warnings war war war.

Collar doves neck and moan   life must go on.

A predatory magpie surveys the scene
and flies away cackling at our dismay.

A flock of waxwings occupies this tree
like the armies massing in the Gulf
are smart in their desert uniforms
as these crested birds are in silhouette.

Late morning. Starlings alight, preen and hop
chatter and squabble, flitter and flutter
take to flight as inconsequentially
as they came. Nerves jangling. Newsflash: War.

Anne Hin

Before sunrise, I consider when waking that

today on the 7-22 from Gypsy Lane to Newcastle
I'm going to sit and really listen to the man
who gets on at Hartlepool, whose breathing's loud
as everything he says, whose laugh's as heavy

as the scuffed NIKE sports bag he always unzips
while he coughs and then rummages for the flask of tea –
where each cup's so sweet, so strong, we all can smell it –
and his bacon butties, always well wrapped in silver foil
in his tupperware container with the loudest of lids,

and his chewed up comments about Sunderland's midfield,
the woeful – and he always repeats the word, woeful – defence,
but I won't let him talk about that.
                              No,
                                    I'll interrupt, ask
about things we may share, an understanding of cats
or garden birds, or the smell of sleeping children, and how
we rarely listen to the way silence can fill us with wonders
that belong to looking at paintings, or hearing music,

and how at night, so many miles apart, we'll each stand
at some open back door and gaze at nothing
but clouds as they hurry overhead, with the empty breeze
seeping through the fence, and then shapes
half-seeable in the darkness that seem like us to belong.

Bob Cooper

Eston Cemetery

(i)

In the new section
Shiny black marble
Colour pictures inset
Of rockin' Elvis Presley
Flash cars and red guitars
Mark the early graves
Of quick young men
Who never will be stars.

(ii)

Walking through the Sixties
Where the shattered sharp edges
Of hammered and battered tombstones
Fallen on the lush body of green grass
Lay where the vandals have cast them;
Living only in the moment of destruction,
Thinking nothing, caring nothing,
Numb with the days of nothing:
This is their silent declaration -
This is their wordless memorial,
The dead man's bones are dust.

(iii)

Turning your pram to shield
Your eyes from the warm Easter sun
Your mind is grabbed at by colour:
The blooming daffodils on older graves
Well-tended flowers on the new arrivals,
William's softly soothing balm of nature;
When I offer you five months old
A stray broken glowing blossom
You reach out grasp and giggle
Beguiled by the newness of yellow.

_)

here is a certain unnamed stillness
ere in the heart of the cemetery
raping old mossy sandstone graves
With no fresh flowers to mark fresh loss,
he ramshackle graffitied chapel
With its aerosol litanies of hate and hurt
om boiling virgins and sad chalk lovers
ecays unmourned in a grey green corner
hough its ancient Norman foundations
nd heavy boned seventeenth century bricks
efuse to rot away to nothing:
he lemon sunlight of blustery March
atches its stones in leaf dappled shadows,

While the weathered markers of iron miners
rumble slowly like the winter minds
f those who can still remember them.

Andy Willoughby

Betrayal

We have a shopping centre, renamed a precinct,
spotted all over with thunderspots of gum.

Cars park on pavements and double yellow lines
so the freeways are clear for the traffic and buggies.

Pathways are a puzzle for dogs guiding the blind
and signposts twirled around mislead the sighted

so they can't find the camping or even the sea.
Plastic crops are collected by volunteer pickers

but no-one is clearing the nettles from the cliffs.
So now I feel guilty and it weighs on my conscience

as heavily as if I had slagged off my grandma
in banner headlines on the front page of *The Sun.*

Pat Brown

Our Beck

Out walking one day,
I saw in the beck
a high back rattan chair.

I wonder who holds council there?

Further on, round a bend,
I found twin beds,
a baby's pram
and several supermarket trolleys.

I know that waterbeds are therapeutic.
More so
with accompanying water music.
I've heard of Water Babies too,
at Malham Tarn, not Marton Beck.

Perhaps they've been transposed.

I wonder who these people are
who live along the beck.
At times
I've even seen a car.

Ruth Ward

the summer fading into spells of

autumn and i pulled away
from this place of low slung buildings,
of trousers tucked in socks and
paradise all around

to alter my head, pull apart me
and replace it with another
that i might return and see
a place that saw fit to bring me about
and the others

those hoards of warrior poets
boiled in the bellies of mad women
the accent that can't be fingered
used to bend the world, surreal
the fighting and the chips
bundled with every lone bedroom
musician, poet and madman

these prophets, these decoders
built from iron, a century and a half
ago, thrown out of doorways, with
dirty water, on cannon street,
shoeless and wrapped in noise

circled by a sleeping beast of hills
left open to explore or ignore
tickled with yellow gorse
and dark seas, request silence
to the right

i return to catch a winter dripping with
heavy moonlight, skies cut
with wing and beak of black and white
the nowists rearranged and love
blossoming, falling, exploding

morning sun through my window
finding a space between the place where
i slept as a child and where nanna died
i'm a son of darkness, who refused to
believe, that was all, from east to west
always running towards patches of sun

and sunsets that most don't see
because they're watching EastEnders
or queuing in KFC
while i wander, ecstatic, monastic around
streets and parks, drinking the instant,
the present, the ground and how it's tied to the pigtails
of the universal now, dragging light
through me and through you and through how

Michael Affleck

Please Take Me Home

Carol, my new friend. We're driving out of
Middlesbrough in the middle of the night.
She's fifty-odd.
Her kids have grown up.
Her whole life just seems completely aimless.
We pass ICI.
Their cooling towers are big fat Buddhas,
moonlit contentment.
Hard to believe they were ever not there.
I tell her I love her.
Of course I mean it.
This is a terrific result for me me me.
Carol is a very lovely lady, a sweetheart.
She may need to be.

John Harrison

Bill's dad at the pub

Regular as clockwork
every night without fail.
Nine o'clock, coat on,
scarf round neck in bad weather,
onward and upward.

Or if not onward and upward,
then a visit to the pub
for four pints – no more, no less.
Lash out on pork scratchings – saves making a proper meal later.
Then home to play on the understrung piano,
drink a cup of Oxo and bed.

Not a bad life, but no way
could you call it a good one.

Carol Cooke

Catherine from Choir

i.m. Cath Dummigan

We'd talk so little singing side by side
even after twenty years I didn't know
the colour, lost young, of her steely hair:
softened and silvering, its careful shape
a cap for delicate features, elfin bones,
compactness. She seemed all in order.
And kind: she would always notice sorrow
unspoken, helping even from her own
last pain.

                    Yet in the breath
given by wild bluebells in our woods, so light
no one can describe it, she is there, or in soft
lilac in our gardens, only known close to.
She is small petals now this colder wind
has parted blown from apple tree and may;
and she is silver still in clouded dawn
holding all the colours of her bright day.

Jo Heather

Note: *Cath Dummigan taught at the University of Teesside
with responsibility for students with disabilities.
The poem was read at a Concert in Stockton Parish
Church in June 2001, a month after her death.*

In Memoriam

Poor Mam, she couldn't work the ethics out:
a truancy which might improve a grade!
"Y'd better tell y' Dad." In case of doubt,
the man must judge and husbands be obeyed.

"I didn't go to school today," I said.
What qualms I had were streaked with flecks of pride.
'I finished *Locksley Hall* and stopped in bed,
revising *Maud*. Last night I put aside

my poetry because we had to do
a diagram of Segment 34
for Common Earthworm Reproduction, too
involved to put the labels on before

we had to stop revising for a Talk
that's called A *Taste for Learning* by a nun
who came from Cambridge with a slice of pork
to stand for Integration, in a bun.

I got behind with Skeletons and Moles.
She said the Hockey Pitch conspires with Art
and Algebra to nourish holy Wholes,
and *Arthur's Death* I didn't even start."

Poor Dad, he'd die before he'd frighten us.
All those unbridled blacksmiths in his blood!
How well he schooled their fire! He didn't fuss,
just mumbled something stern and vaguely good.

Poor Mam, so richly blessed and all agog
to guess the big Surprise I'd 'phoned about:
a Bursary derived from mud and fog
to write about her husband catching trout.

Now if he'd known – Lord Tennyson, I mean –
his trustees' protégée would fail him twice
at Level 'O', would he have been so keen?
The moral maze of this was far too nice

to ask the Doctor. Would the Vicar do?
Dad's gone to Heaven where such things are clear.
I greased her crippled hands with what she knew
I'd hid behind my back to melt her fear.

Her eyes may open now. It is allowed
in Paradise to peep through little holes
this heavy fat has made in that thick shroud
as though it were the oil to do with souls.

Above the scentless webs of deft debates
her messy Gorgonzola celebrates.

Epilogue

Beyond the gym, the everlasting hills
stand up and take the morning to the plains
Oenone fades to colour, wilting wills
her evensong trains tall with supple canes.

Unmarked in fusing clouds, the Cleveland hills awake,
imagining their mysteries are mist.
The simple chimes o'er dappled dells for Break
will rhyme with severed subjects on a list.

Norah Hi

Language

For Joseph Woods

You tell me in your language
there's a word for that loneliness
felt at cock crow. I tell you
in mine there's one for sorrow
on a station platform, late Sunday afternoon.
Mine has one for a woman
who cries at funerals and christenings alike,
and you say the name yours gives
to a final night together
when this fact's known to one
but not the other.

Yours, you claim, has 500 terms for rain.
I can't beat that!
But can reel off more than fifty
for the different consistencies of slurry.

Then you reveal to me what you'd call
a get well note in the post,
with the mail van in the lane
pulling over for the hearse.
So I confide to you my abstract noun
for that feeling at the back of the head
of a heavy door closing to.
You say it sounds a little like
a verb you know for the motion described
by a high-wire artist in mid-fall
without a net. Yes, I explain,
both come from the same archaic stem
as that for a tap which has jammed full on.

Katharine Banner

The Irish word *iarmhaireacht* is translated in Dineen's Irish – English
Dictionary as:
the state of being remnant or reduced; loneliness, the loneliness felt at
cock crow.

37

The year Peggy-Sue got married

My mother could have married an Irishman-
a stout black and white fellow, with sideburns,
who played guitar.

She shows me the autograph book
of pictures of the lady who would have been my nan.
His brothers and sisters, the rest of his band,
they are all in a row, squinting at the sun,
outside chalky low houses.
Underneath he has written in flowing penmanship
"My lovely, when will you come?"

I know the story. She was seventeen.
Her best friend was Maureen,
who she told everything,
except when she sent the card saying
Weather is good. Food is too much.
People are great. I am not coming home.

In a leatherette vanity case with pleated red satin innards
my mother keeps four postcards of houses
and churches by the sea, a sunset.
A wooden cross he bought her, a three-leaf clover.
A skeleton of a sycamore leaf,
a brass money box shaped like a book
and a snakeskin album of the man
she says looks like Buddy Holly,
plenty of empty pages for when she goes back.

Angela Readman

No Papers

for Fiston Lusambo

A pleated skirt of terraced houses
The wind's whiskers in the gaps

You're numbed

by the cold. In a fine house a fire burns
red and bronze

If you lean against the walls you feel
the heat

You can't go there to fetch embers
They'll ask to see your papers

Play your guitar with broad hands
No one knows about your home land

Let your eyes sparkle; strum soft
songs. Your feet hardly move a notch

Just a slight shift of the hips

The crowd slips off as
the music dies. Cold and embarrassed

You slip through the silence
back to iced apartments
with the rhythm flaming in your fingers.

Pauline Plummer

His Hands

Big hands, strong fingers, salt soaked,
Sore from hauling pots and lines.
Wrists rubbed raw by oilskins chafing.
Muscular arms, shoulders and back
From pulling oars, heaving nets.
Strong legs set wide apart to counter
The roll and pitch of boat beneath,
Seaboot-clad feet.
Hands capable of sculling with a single oar
Or feathering it so lightly
That salmon would almost leap into his net.
Strong hands with a vice-like grip.
Yet gentle, so gentle, to bear a child aloft,
To carry him shorewards, through treacherous surging tides,
Across sea-washed scaurs and beaches
In the sheltered bay, between high cliffs
That lie along this rock-strewn coast.
Amidst all the vagaries of the weather,
Through sun-kissed days and black stormy nights.
To carry his son safely home.
His hands bear testimony to his past,
Big hands, strong hands, scarred hands
From salt water boils, fillet knife slashes,
Rope burns when he paid out a line too quickly,
When he was young.
When he could splice a rope, tie a knot, weave a net, bait a line
With his strong, nimble, dextrous, fine-tuned hands,
Capable of any task they were set.
These skills he learned from his father
He would pass on to his sons.

Keith Porri

My Name is Mark and

after Charles Bernstein

am a northern poet, a northwestern poet,
a northeastern poet, a Stockton poet,
a Preston poet, a Teesside poet,
a domestic poet, a political poet,
an evasive poet, a formal poet, an ex-
perimental poet, a reflective poet, a strategic poet,
a part-time poet, an evenings and weekends poet,
a 24 hour party poet, a performance poet,
a preschool poet, a streetwise poet,
a smart arse poet, a wry poet,
a real poet, a male poet, a people's poet,
a blue poet, a red poet, a green poet,
a black-white-and-read-all-over poet,
a ready made poet, a donkey of a poet,
am a love poet in the morning,
a darkly comic poet over lunch,
a post-prandial second language poet,
a crispy edge of the lasagne poet at teatime,
a pop poet watching the telly,
and an interrogative poet in the sack,
am a creative poet, a restricted poet,
a poet making the most of slender means,
a listed poet, a candidate poet,
a could-have-been-a-contender poet,
a young poet, a poet with a maturing voice,
a gritty poet, a can-I-take-it-to the-bridge-
yeah-go-on-take-it-to-the-bridge poet,
an anti-poet, a poet who hates beauty
for its own sake and its own good,
a poet after Auschwitz and the poet who
put the ram in the ramalamadingdong,
am a vernacular poet, a poet
of exquisite juxtapositions,
a poet inhabited by inhibition,
am a poet with a mission,
a missionary poet with a million positions,
a beat poet, jazz poet, spoken word poet,
am an ironic poet, a post-punk poet,
a just-add-boiling-water poet,
a poet with attitude, a fraudulent poet,
a situationist poet, a dead poet,

a situation-communist poet,
I am an accessible poet, I am a poet
banging a tambourine, I am a poet with a headache
backache and an indefinable langour,
a terminal case of ennui,
I am a discursive poet, a generative poet,
an imagist who scorns the sketch,
a research poet, a poet ever puzzled,
a product poet, a process poet,
I am a terraced house poet, a pacifist
terrorist poet with a pillowful of feathers,
an erotic poet, a dream poet, a dream-song-sung-blue poet,
a poet without a home, a poet in his place,
a poet crying for mother and apple pie,
a stir-fried tofu poet, a white bread black pudding poet,
I am a poet in the field, a poet at large,
a systems poet, a computer generated poet,
a small press poet, a hard pressed poet,
a depressed poet, a suppressed poet,
a poet reeling with surprise and delight,
a husband poet, son poet, brother poet,
dad poet, a dadaist poet, a sudden movement poet,
a martian poet, a poet behaving badly,
a talkin-'bout-my-generation poet,
a post-post-post-post-post poet,
a modernist poet in the market place,
a gnomic poet on the street corner,
a never-going-to-be-on-the-South-Bank-Show poet,
a tea-time local news poet, a tense poet,
a speak my weight poet, an eat my words poet,
an educated poet, a philistine poet,
an aesthetic principles don't butter the bread poet,
a poetry boom revival poet, a dusty corner poet,
a dictionary poet, a tip of the tongue poet,
a poet in a mess, a you-hum-it-I'll-play-it poet,
a stop-this-poem-I-want-to-get-off poet.

Mark Robinson

Gaps

She smoked cigarettes four at a time
The first time I really knew I'd seen her,
In the playground she played football with the boys,
Fought and swore but could be quiet as a murmur

In the days before sunlight could be
Transformed into some idea of freedom
We walked together saying nothing or joking;
When one of the horses in the fields off the estate

Broke free she cried for it being run over:
The nervous kicking quick black hoofing
Left us as wordless as the endless stream
Of numbness that soaked us to the bone

With feelings unspoken with words redundant
On a red brick estate where our fathers
Drank themselves silent on Friday nights
Or exhausted from work demanded silence

"ve nowt to do with culture
So let me watch the snooker"
That desperate need for order
In a world of work and food and family

She had given up her smoking the last time that I saw her,
We both had words we never knew when we first met,
But despite the clever way we filled the gaps,
There was more in the silences that we left.

Andy Willoughby

Another place

Everyone was talking
like an orchestra forever tuning up,
and I thought of a place we used to go
and I might find a sign of you, a silk square
or the circle your finger might trace in my palm,
but there were only bits of your shadow left
among fallen leaves coming to life
in the sudden pulse of a breath of wind
like the leavings of a garden fire.

John Brelstaf

Post Script At Skinningrove

And after the fishing you might have been a bidder
going from house to house announcing funerals.
They would have known you by your apron, gift
from the bereaved.

Or you could have been a waiter,
leading the procession from grave to tea
and ham sandwiches. They would know you
by white armbands on your black, white gloves
when you handed out spiced loaf
and cheese.

You could have been the midwife
holding newborn aloft above your head,
or anxious mother with a whooping baby,
catching whiffs of shot-firing at the drift
entrance.

You would have dreaded a howling dog,
a bird tapping at the window, a crowing hen
and anything that came in threes.
Never would you put new shoes on the table,
so much like laying out a corpse in boots
and just as easily come by down the mine
as out at sea.

Pat Brown

My Great Aunt Cis

In the album, a fashion plate at forty,
with everything held in,
crushed pansy face and prim.
A spinster of this parish.
The family set her up in "Gowns,
an agent for Spirella."
She lived above the shop on Linthorpe Road,
her watercolours on the wall,
a drawing room piano.
Behind the spectacles, jet beads,
she had something up her costume sleeve.

How they met, I've no idea
or when Irish Uncle Tom moved in.
For me he'd always been there,
rough tweed against her crepe de chine,
his growling dog under the table.

At the back of the shop
she measured, and kept secrets;
with neat feet treadled away,
her mouth drawn tight with pins.
She gave me velvets and brocades
to dress my dolls,
scraps of richness.

Shirley Hetheringto

Unlettered

It startled me a bit, that plaque, at first.
A little story on a garden wall!
So many words! It made me think of plums,
unstinting, wandered through an orchard fence.

How strange to think of children living here.
They never saw the vicar's knobbly knees;
the salmon paste in buns on paper plates;
the daisy slope we rolled down after tea.

I didn't know all this: what happened when
the Sisters left. We often wondered that.
They seemed to vanish with the crested gate
gallant with flags; the coconuts; the shy

St. Oswald's Scouts fixed up behind the lake.
The chiselled words explain. How good to know
it didn't fizzle out, that little Guild.
It isn't what you'd think they'd go in for,

those quiet nuns, not open much to change.
Perhaps they got took over. Anyhow,
it seems they run a kind of Healing Home.
Poets and painters do the counselling.

Another thing I never knew – (The words,
them lovely deep incisions, clean and grave,
all sorts they've taught me, tucked below the hedge) –
before the Convent – (probably the fêtes

paid for those annexes the Sisters built) –
a smaller house stood here – still big, of course:
an ironmaster's mansion known for miles.
Twelve maids they had and seven gardeners.

That lettering: it says a lot, does that.
The Housing Trust that bought the site. It shows
there's more to them than profit, that and how
they've blended them new flats with that old stone.

That metal page speaks volumes – (Just a way
of speaking; just a turn of phrase that comes
when something brings it back like snatches of
a tune) – and yet it's books behind all this:

a woman in a story I once read.
Dismembered. A librarian: a rape
set in some ancient culture: evil hordes.
It wasn't drunks that smashed the gentle bulge,

them convex sentences that clothed the curve.
Banners they seemed to me, like Blake's on brick:
them windy ribbons, undulating scrolls,
writing not separate from the static paint.

It took electric drills to crack that steel.
The lovely information's in the mud.
A chunk of background tore my sandal strap.
The grout's not solid, somehow, shaved of ghosts.

It's dirty, this. I know because the blank,
it seems to make the garden party clothes –
those frilly hems you had to starch – so limp.
Some energy to do with holiness:

this nothing says it isn't really there.
This coldness could unfrock the summer skirts,
the dancing on the grass, the skipping race.
I thought, "I must lie down in the clean moon.

If I lie still, those instruments will come,
redemptive horns a priest knows how to hold."
I thought it out. I would avenge her death,
that lady I'd forgot about in books.

What vigour comes with it, this holy oil,
I cannot understand! It spurts like milk.
The ice upon the axe, the melting sting
of toffee apples in a silly tent

I have been saddled with. They shall be yoked.
Surely this yoke is easy. "Yes", I thought.
No call for me to tell why, meaning this
good work, no welding sparked the gloom apart.

What I have left undone, though, I won't vow
a simple silence over. Grace to sing

that takes away abduction, took me on;
plagued gods to fray a bond's exhausted due;

passed over old arrangements to the chief
Musician, notes with fresh instructions on:
more lovely than before, unfractured words;
pied pipes to bring them home instead of rats.

It wasn't false, the rhymed lament I meant.
A flaw has got itself into the score:
in a plain trellis, convoluted fret
we could stray in and out of, glimpsing fruit.

I have a son – grown up, of course. He rang.
He said, "I'm coming through. We're going out."
He said, "I'll take you for a Birthday meal."
A lovely place we went to near the hills.

That figured dress he sent me years ago,
I put it on to please him, but the belt,
It's got too tight. I had to take it off.
I said, "That food – the heat – the crowded room –

"Thank heaven for the dark!" Unbuckled gold,
made us giggle on the sleepy green.
I said, "We must walk miles in this bright moon."
The happy kiss, the wine at ancient inns;

The jokey arm around the empty loops
corral no shame's unbridled solitude.
How frail the plough, its starry embryo;
the sleeping ducks; the daffodils become

narcissi in the moon where I can reach
almost, the coming courtesy of plums;
the spikes they dangle through, the lichened rails
the vanished children climb to peer across;

the joined beasts pulling well; a furrow's scan.

Norah Hill

Note: *the plaque commemorated the existence of the Nunnery on this site in Marton Road, Middlesbrough.*

The Cake

My cousin's husband's mother got cancer,
Quite young,
My cousin went to help her father-in-law
Sort through the clothes
Boil an egg
Tidy the cupboards, that sort of thing.

She found a cake in a tin in the kitchen,
It glowed with fruit and candied peel,
It spiced the air with cinnamon and ginger
And brandy,
It had been baked for Christmas
And was set aside to mature,
Ripening nicely,
As poison spread elsewhere -
An unwelcome advent
That fogged the windows
And shut down the calendar early.

It was said that, at the end,
She lost her mind,
Before she lost her body,
But some of her actions
Are open to interpretation –
We are told it was not a happy marriage,
There was talk of an affair.

At the funeral tea
My cousin thought it would be nice
To serve the cake,
Sylvia's farewell gift
To all who mourned her.

My cousin took the big knife and sliced in,
Releasing the delicious odours,
Revealing the cherries and raisins,
The sultanas and peel,
The buttery, sugary wholesomeness

And also the pins
That ran right through.

Rowena Sommervil

50

Sunday Overtime 1939

The Bakery was hot
and half in the dark
as I sat on a chair swinging my legs
in the gloom
whilst Dad sweated
in the melting heat
under the glass half-roof.

Grains of flour, powder-fine and stifling,
hung in the air
as he sifted it for the short-crust pastry.
Up to his elbows,
he mixed in the eggs and water
before shaping and rolling it
for Maids of Honour.

The smell of the almondy filling
reminded me of the garden at home
on a summer's afternoon
like this one,
the melted jam only adding
to the cacophony
of remembered tastes.

Mollie Hill

Jalepeno's, Extra Cheese

Pull open a Stella,
I ask how many she's been with.
Shake up the can, till all the fizz is gone;
Flat. She answers with question.
"Been what? _Naked? _To sleep? To the movies?"

"Lovers."

Bends her fingers back, she lists all the lads
she ever kissed. Names like Ste, Andy, Gary,
sink plunging lips, signing their autographs
with sand tongues.
"How did they love me?" she says,
 "Let me count the ways...None."

Watching Ricki Lake she slits her wrists;
open mouthed smiles on her skin
her fingers make talk.
"It was just to see the bones moving"
she says, "I'm hungry, starving, bored."

Bound her up in a faded Lou Reed T-shirt,
ordered pizza and hired *American Werewolf in London*.
One eye on special effects, in bed I asked her.
She said she wanted to see what was in her,
see how she worked, before she stopped.

Angela Readma.

n Bilsdale 2001

to a friend (whom I will ring again)

Rain at last. We'd forgotten
what loud rain, heavier grey light, can do
o summer. Artists find green difficult, but these fields
re impossible: saturated, solid,
andelion and broom shout
ke too much mustard, farm-roofs' oranges
not in drably, and knapweed's a blue
o green should ever be seen out with.
ot tapestry, but a tanktop knitted
or someone not quite loved enough.

urn from the glass: even sure-footed cattle, so
lack and white, this year lack all certainties.
witch onto lamplight and the stove's
plump red pepper, your walls' colour
arm as strawberries. Layer
atisfied ironing tall; when the phone thrills
nswer. Best of all
n with your daughter's wedding cake:
e fruit is ready, brandy-surfeited.
ift. Stir. Pour.

Jo Heather

Middlesbrough Pride
the name of a rose

'It's pink and fragrant,' said the gardener's boy.
I had to smile at the catalogue-speak,
the sack wrapped bolus he held out to me
gave no such promise, its blackened branches
cut hard back.   Bred, not for the pride,
that's patronising marketing, but to survive
in uncertain climates and poor soils
yet still grow beautiful.
If colour and fragrance can be described with words,
then it's all the changes in a sunset
and a perfume I could breathe away.
Not a hot house flower to bring indoors,
the petals will open too soon and fall,
it's an all weather rose that thrives in clay
and blooms until December.

Ann O'Ner

Oh let there be blossom,

let the Malteser packets, Carlsberg cans, bonbon wrappers,
with all the brightness of their colours get hidden by the
        suddenness,
let the Sainsbury polybag trees bud and turn cherry pink or
        white
and hedges whose blackthorn starkness seems aggressive
pple themselves with the palest of green. Let there be blossom
o even the two old men who silently pad along together –
ne with a dog as withdrawn as each other – pause and talk
uietly about something that makes them smile as they look.
let the refuse trucks rust and orange slab sides gleam with
        petals,
he woman who tries to sweep them from her path stop and
        start to grin.
let there be blossom that flavours the air like chilli powder
avours what bubbles in pans in kitchens still gleaming with
        sunlight
while the radio plays love songs and mothers sing, revealing
o themselves such secrets that are coloured in such lyrics
while they stir, tap the rim with a rhythm they're hardly aware of
s they mouth every *Aaah*, every *Oh*, then smile to themselves.

Bob Cooper

Inventing the tenses

We have taken to it
like ducks to champagne
inventing the mythic tenses
paddling and breasting
with a duck-billed smile
swirls of our rivery story.

None of us wants to
remember
the past indefinite
its ripped fish
its muddy bottoms
glass-eyed
we let all that drop in the drink.

But all look forward to
the future imperfect
its well-quacked failings
its cork-tight excuses
champagne off ducks' backs.

We could have pointed out
but lack fingers
the pluperfect indicative
as over and done with
long before ducks were involved
no doubt things were better
than now and here's sorrows
anyway bottoms up
not worth drowning over.

Though soon downstream
of us
the present inedible
is more of a challenge
to our bubbly
inventiveness
we argue endlessly
stabbing and chewing
its white slices
its plastic packaging
knowing it is bad for us.

Could get used though to this
subordinate imperative
like ducks to the laughter
inking each other
and without tears.

Gordon Hodgeon

Rough sleeper/We are stardust

Thank God we live in the north.
Not many rough sleepers here, too cold really.
Better off in Bath, Bristol,
or London, where there's loads of them.
Better off with their own kind, not cluttering up my street,
making the place untidy, making me feel uncomfortable.

Because when you look at it,
they're not like you and me.
Are they?

Astrophysicists and molecular biologists beg to differ.
We all carry heavy elements inside.
Phosphorus, iron, carbon,
helium and hydrogen - making stars,
which don't hang about for ever,
but explode, scatter and form planets.

Our bodies, made from rogue stars and planets.
Dead stars.
All of us – dead stars.

Carol Cook

Dante's Leopard
(See Inferno, I, 32 : Jorge Luis Borges)

A leopard, in a Borges parable,
Caged in a Florentine duecento zoo,
Dreams of there being some purpose in its pain –
To seed a dozen lines of epic verse:
It cannot grasp the workings of the world …

Banished from Florence for his politics,
The poet Dante dreams that his despair –
Commuted into the *Commedia* –
Will be remembered in another age:
He cannot grasp the workings of the world …

While, in his Buenos Aires library,
Borges himself, sequestered by ill-health,
Living only through the mirror of his books,
Weaves Dante's thread into his web of thought
And strives to grasp the workings of the world.

The butterfly of Chaos Theory,
By fluttering its iridescent wings,
Creates a whirlwind half a world away.
Schopenhauer counterposes two wild beasts,
One avidly devouring the other,
To illustrate the ratio of pain
To pleasure in this state of dog-eat-dog.

The prodigality of misery
Means that the outcome will be much the same
Whether we are resistant or resigned:
Jorge Luis Borges, a butterfly,
A flailing victim of the sudden storm,
A savage predator, a savaged prey,
Dante Alighieri, or a leopard.

J. Chesterfield

Stardust

In this fragile world
Poisonous tensions divide
Stardust from stardust.

How shall we respond?
Reflect starry origins,
Be anti-toxic!

Recognise kinship
Celebrate variety
Light up a bright sky.

Rowena Sommervill

At a certain hour

Ask me at the right hour,
and I will spill   over
the secret content of shadow.
I will show my favourite light when I elongate.
We overlap till it is evening.

By the Eight till Late,
I cannot see the constellations.
Orion, Hunter, his Belt, the Plough
are spilt as glitter over paste.
And the rain is a lacquer on you
Solid, cool,
more silver than a CD moon.

Ask, on certain nights the Cosmos
seems so small, I can hardly read the blurred carbon copy.
And I've almost counted the stars,
accessed every one in a blink.
I ask the sky, I've dusted clouds
wished on ha'penny planets, pocketed a smile.

I've almost touched you.

You eclipse
into neon, and I catch the steamy dusk.
og of day, tread your satellite;
gravity weightless   float
nameless
is the third man in your space

Angela Readman

Somnambulist

1.

Somewhere between midnight and day
Neighbour downstairs turns
The lock in her door.
I'm reminded of the late hours
Dad stayed out,
Lying in bed with my sisters,
Wondering where he had been,
Wishing that I
Had the same liberty.

2.

She's lost us both,
Mother is searching in the woods.
We are here, sleeping next to you,
But she's frightened.
Little one was always lost to us all
Playing in her own world.
And now I have also gone
Too far to find my way back.

3.

On awakening this morning, the earth trembled,
Teesside trembled too last night.
And those with whom
I had spent 22 years
Shook their heads at me.
Far from those terraced housed streets
I look out of the window
To see another blue sky,
The *Boulangerie* down the road has opened.
I wonder what the weather is like
In England.

Ghazala Bash

Last Night

Tonight, on the balcony that has hardly room
for a chair, in a long lilac breeze, a cicada somewhere
squeezes the night. Old men of Café Sporte shuffle
dominoes around veneer, and cough with a good
smoker's hack. Tomorrow, I take an early flight.
Ready to smile at the smog-trails of Middlesbrough,
when my train trundles in from Thirsk. To greet the frowns
of commuters, the slouches of my fellow Ingles
pressed to low cloud; to queues of letters, and post-its;
and feel the pull to the sight of your upside down eyes.
Tomorrow, I fly home on an early flight, but tonight
I'll write, listening to Senor Cicada from across the road,
the bark of an ancestral dog pack scouring the river side.

Bob Beagrie

Mudfog Declares War on Tourism

The Mayor of Mudfog said today
  He pledged his full support
To fight the Tourists all the way,
And would outlaw without delay
  Hawaiian shirt and shorts.

'No hiding place for Tourists here!'
  The Mayor of Mudfog cried,
'Our way of life will disappear,
The values that we most hold dear,
  If we just stand aside.'

The Tourist menace thus was met
  With Anti-Tourist laws,
To stop the foreign Tourist threat
And catch all those within the net
  Who live beyond these shores.

We started burning A-Zs
  And outlawed phrase-book phrases,
And burned the Tourists in their beds
And shot all those with crew-cut heads
  And sent them all to blazes.

We stopped the evil Tourist lot
  And shackled them in chains,
We smashed their cameras on the spot
To make quite sure that they would not
  Try Tourism again.

And now that they have run away
  And all the world is glad,
The Mayor of Mudfog left today
To start a five week holiday
  In Kabul and Baghdad.

Andy Cro

The Elephants of Mudfog

As the sun climbed up over the chimneys,
  And the traffic jams started to crawl,
Ten stone elephants marched into Mudfog
  And sat down beside the Town Hall.

Now nobody knew where they came from,
  Or what they were hoping to do,
Perhaps they'd escaped from a circus?
  Perhaps they belonged in a zoo?

A terrified crowd quickly gathered
  And stared at the marvellous sight,
Ten stone elephants sitting in Mudfog -
  It shouldn't be, couldn't be right !

Then someone alerted the council,
  Who called out the National Guard,
Who called for a SWAT team and air-strike,
  (Cos shooting an elephant's hard).

The elephants stared at the soldiers
  And blinked in the bright Mudfog sun,
Until a small child ran over and smiled
  And gave one a Greggs' currant bun.

The crowd watched in silent amazement
  As the elephant picked up the lad,
Then stood to its feet and walked down the street
  And brought him back safe to his dad.

Hurrah for the mammoths of Mudfog!
  Three cheers for our elephant chums!
Although it's well known that they're just made of stone
  Their hearts are as big as their bums.

They soon were a local attraction,
  They even gave rides to the Mayor,
Folk came from afar, by coach and by car,
  To stare at them sat in the square.

They starred in a *Blue Peter* special,
  They handed out gongs at the Brits,
Took part in another new round of Big Brother,
  And modelled the new England kits ;

There was talk of a remake of Dumbo,
  The National Lottery draw,
The rumours were thick of a *Hannibal* pic,
  A phone-in on Radio 4.

The jumbos were quite a sensation,
  They helped put the place on the map;
Some artists came down to visit the town
  In search of some elephant crap.

But alas, there were some folk in Mudfog
  Who resented the elephants' fame,
Their lives were so grim and their brains were so dim,
  And they needed somebody to blame.

They stood in the Mudfog elections
  And ranted and raved on the telly,
'You've got to be firm with a stone pachyderm,
  Our watchword is *Not on Your Nelly!'*.

'We'll be swamped,' said their Florida spokesman,
  'They're animals under the skin,
Once they've heard we're a soft touch in Mudfog
  We'll have herds of them trying to get in!'

Each night in the town's evening paper
  The letters were worried and vexed,
'It's time our friend Ganesh was taught how to vanish,
  Or else it's our jobs will be next.'

Some said that their skin was too wrinkled,
  Or else that their trunks were too long,
Unnatural, alien, not local to Mudfog -
  In short that they didn't belong.

The council proposed a solution
  Which they hoped would help sort out the mess,
They gave them permission to stay on condition
  That they tried to stand out a bit less.

Do you have to be such a strange colour?
  Do elephants have to be tall?
Could your trunks be a little bit briefer?
  And why can't your ears be more small?

To be honest, those tusks are just wasted
  On creatures with no sense of price,
Your bums require slimming, your toe-nails need trimming,
  And to eat with your nose isn't nice.

We know you've a right to be different,
  We respect this, as everyone does,
But they say, 'When in Rome', so now Mudfog's your home,
  Why can't you become more like *us*?'

The elephants listened in silence
  Then they turned and walked slowly away,
And the only reminder they came here at all
  Is that Mudfog's now elephant grey.

Andy Croft

Beyond Clichés

on Saltburn beach

a lonely sandwich and the black dog
and my dead Mum hanging round a lot

and the Saturday surfers   wet suit legs
torsos as hard and young as new winter weather

imagine this weather, the worst weather
for a picnic on the dunes

it was the kind of light that drained all colour
scenery grubby and nothing vivid

except my black dog mood
high tides had washed a lot of sand away

cliffs had slid   turf bunched up at the foot
like the scalded skin of Howard's arm that slipped

down the bone to gather around his wrist
in a soggy bracelet   sea, rough and grey

I had my eyes cast down, studying the shore
then I looked up   it was over the sea

a complete bow   all the colours and more
light so bright it silvered the breakers

inside the bow, sky like old varnish on an old master
outside the bow, the sky was darker

it was like a Gateway to a Golden World
the pier   wet black   a path through

anglers kept fishing, surfers surfed faster
gamblers in the amusements played on

as the light moved   Huntcliff's fields
were painted gold and the murky buildings

caravans, trees   of the seafront town
stood black against its ethereal glow

in all that wet, I was dry and warm
and the ocean rushed and roared with laughter.

Marilyn Longsta

Am Somewhere Else

A sombre day for us, we are at odds, two
ungainly giants reaching out on a white beach in sunshine.
Rainbow-coloured people scatter like ants.
Huntcliff saws into blue, a shark's huge tooth.
We once met a stranger who jumped from that cliff:
he looked into your eyes and she flew.
I write on sand, 'Whatever dies was not mix't equally'.
You are the only man I know who hasn't read John Donne,
who couldn't kill a gnat, who'll lift me up.

Safe in the town we choose a silvery ring
twining with knots that don't quite tally.
Another window shows old photographs,
Saltburn, Brotton, Loftus, Hinderwell, Staithes:
flocks of people on streets and beaches, not unhappy,
wearing heavy clothes, totally black, not moving.

Jo Heather

Treasurers

(For Cath and Bill)

'Clay is the word and clay is the flesh'
(Patrick Kavanagh, *The Great Hunger*)

Where the treasure gatherers live
along the old fall of the Tees,
listen for an hour, have they anything to give
of life as it is, boarded up and on its knees?

There is a light of imagination in this road
of anonymous houses where numbers must be asked.
We quiver at wound-down windows,
clammy steering wheels in our rigid grasp.

Here, a man so loves the blue grain of the land,
he scours the beck with a metal detector;
returns with clay pipes and yesterday's glass in his hand;
Stockton bottles, Stevens ink-wells, musket balls, marble
            chequers

She's already unearthed the treasure of Giggy Moon,
gives you a cup of tea, tells you not to let it get cold.
She knows what she knows.
Jimmy James was her Godfather.

Maureen Almon

Midnight Ploughing

Over your shoulder
the six-furrow reversible
you felled a mid-field tree
to make a clear way for,
promising a forest
in a *better* place,
is turning up
new clutches of stones.

Stubble folds against the trash board
and is gently buried and though
it's doubtful cut worms can forgive
you argue that in time
each part will realign
self with gravity;
that even the shaken stones
will soon bed down again.

Reaching the headland
you begin the turn,
raise the hydraulics
and swing the plough:
it lifts an eyebrow,
catches sight of the moon
and chances a wink
at its namesake constellation.

Katharine Banner

Aerial Photography

The flight path diagram
records those moments in August '88
when a tight-shuttered camera blinked
and thought it had conjured
a world outside itself.

Each triangle translates
to fields and lanes and buildings.
Frame two four three expatiates:
skims a hundred acres of stubble
and then, abruptly, offers up
an odd-shaped mound, or hollow;
a copse beside a white-rimmed lake;
a darker patch – high water, or cloud shadow.

A combine part way through a field of corn
is broken down, or working;
a dot on a driveway's arriving, or leaving.
And with my magnifying glass
I find, on a track
which from the ground
I once believed I knew,
two spots, like flicked ink, merging.

Slow planes, which take
such long range views,
passed overhead, as unremarked-upon
that summer as any other,
which likely saw,
as every summer sees,
its share of accidents, or rendezvous.

Katharine Banne

Not Quite Good Enough

ɔ eat, there's a thread in this morning
ɦat I will hold onto
while my descant ploughs it to mud.
owhere is as nowhere does,
s shape at the back of my throat
 cry, grain, a frayed response soon
wordless,

l texture and no text,
 the sunlight or the rain,
e gap between truth and harmony,
ow and here two halves of nowhere.

Mark Robinson

Loose connections beneath the dashboard

From Yarm to Netherthong on an empty tank
without adding a mile to our history,
we have guessed our speed in the suburbs,
crossed our fingers in sweaty gridlock
and cruising on the M1 listened to rattles
accumulate like guilty verdicts,
first one sorry hand, then another,
then more until it's unanimous: off with his head.
According to the car we have not moved.
The landscape was having us on,
tugging hedgerows into the distant behind-us,
the wheels were turning in air, or mud,
and this holiday cannot yet have started -
the children are still screaming to leave.
But the momentum that carried us here
must register somewhere. The wheels
could draw a map or a house or a face
without turning the clock or taking a pound,
without scratching our part-exchange,
but something has shifted, has pushed us
99 miles towards older and wiser.
Repeating this trick is a difficult knack,
one that can get you from yesterday
to now to tomorrow and back.

Mark Robins‹

Waiting

so that I hate my youth's long day –
the grave's rest still so far!

Late January, under the church wall's height
the snowdrops struggle out, their papery white
as sparse and pale as hairs left in my head.
Their anchors are the chalked bones of the dead.

The year that's gone, so far from what we guessed,
the worst much worse, the good far from the best,
the new graves not those that we had predicted,
our choice of plot by these that much restricted.

Now, as the footpaths open up and stick
swings round and thwacks to raise the bramble's sneck,
the gales sweep in and turn the fields to flood,
the resurrected sheep are fleeced in mud.

These summaries of day in winter's long
and whining tenebrae, that lights-out song,
these snowdrops rise, their paper white as bone,
brief IOUs, on which I could write down

the debts I owe you, love, this time of year
when hope and joy get trampled under fear,
attraction shrinks all shrivelled in the cold
and passion hugs its blanket damp with mould.

The dead beat grasses lying in my way
will lift their seed-heads to the longest day,
so everything will come to one who waits
with fading snowdrops by the churchyard gates.

Gordon Hodgeon

New Ghosts

By field, forest, seacliff, scarp and moor
with many a track and bridlepath
tied together like any old bits of string,
we walk the thread of the Cleveland Way
in a wild-weather company of monks,
drovers, merchants, pilgrims, panniermen

and now, on sections newly flagged
with floorstones from old Bradford mills,
children, who trod them, calling each other
through the clattering storm of the looms.

John Brelsta.

Launch Day at Furness Shipyard c1968

Painted high on hammered iron
Exotic names are washed in wine
Worthy of the trades
Who transformed molten juice
Into Greek legend.

Monica Sharp

Ghost Town

The town I inhabit is
sootier, smaller, safer.
I can reach out and touch the sides.
Iron masters and shop keepers its elite,
but gritty men who worked the foundries and shipyards
were its mainstay.
My great granddad, it is said,
tiled the roof of our Town Hall
and on the wall of Albert Park
my soldier uncle's name stands proud.
We prized our Meccano bridges,
the cafe with a Burmese room,
our football ground
and Dorman Museum
whose stuffed and scabby lion
stalked so many of our dreams.
Here we lifted covers from glass cases
to reveal treasures,
dappled birds' eggs, exotic shells.
The sheen of butterflies' wings.
We didn't believe them
when they said this colour was an illusion,
only refracted light.

Shirley Hetheringtc

eaning on his shovel
On the furnace floor.
A Cargo Fleet smelter.

weat towel draped about his neck.
lue bottle glass specs
hoved high on his forehead.

is balding head glistening.
e listens, feels, hears
he furnace song.

he loud roaring of hot blast,
he plip-plopping tinkling sound
f steel and slag boiling.

e raises the furnace door.
iews the fiery interior.
ees the smelt boil.

rders the chargers in,
undling down the steel shop floor,
uckets full of alloying elements.

harge forward into the all-consuming heat.
otate bucket, spill contents.
to the seething mass.

ithdraw hastily, beat a retreat
efore shaft and bucket begin to melt.
hen down the shop floor for another load.

he smelter leads his gang, starts the round,
hey walk in a circle, loose limbed,
hovels hanging on extended arms.

ees sag, thrust forward, scoop.
ft arm as pivot, thrust down with right.
raighten up, walk up to furnace door.

ant feet firmly, sway of hips, swing arms,
uck shovel load right to the back of the furnace.
hovel after shovel of limestone spread

Over boiling, spitting metal,
Providing a blanket of flux
To ease out impurities.

This limestone a week ago a rockface in a quarry,
in Wensleydale.
Now turned liquid, floating on top of molten metal.

Heat is energy sapping.
He drinks a lot
To make up for the sweat oozing
From every pore of his body.

Steel has many alloys.

Chromium,
            Manganese,
                        Molybdenum,
                                    Mild,
                                          Carbon,
                                                Tool.

All require different formulae.
All have different melting points.

He must know when
To add various elements
To increase or decrease temperature.

Add flux.
Pour. To tilt massive furnace.
Run off slag, carefully.

To leave his smelt unadulterated.
To teem it into ingots
To be later rolled into

Blooms,
        Billets,
                Joists,
                        Beams,
                                Channels,
                                        Piles,
                                                Angles,
                                                      Flats
                                                            and T Bar
To be
Sent to the far ends of the earth.

Keith Por

Steel Giant Threatens to Quit Mudfog

There once was a very big giant,
  A fairy-tale giant of steel,
He was built by a hard-working people
  To safeguard their town's commonweal.

They'd heard tales of the capital city
  Where the money-faced monsters lurk
That feed upon small towns like Mudfog,
  Devouring their wages and work.

So they laboured to build their colossus,
  And they struggled a century and more,
By day and by night the skies were alight
  With the bright burning hopes of the poor.

They fed it with coal and with iron,
  And they sweetened its brow with their sweat,
They worked and they toiled and they polished and oiled
  Till they thought the steel giant in their debt.

And its legs were as long as a late shift,
  It was hard as a job in the mills,
Its heart was as hot as a furnace,
  Its memory was old as the hills.

But the day came, alas, when the giant
  Decided the town was too small,
For a giant needs gold and adventure
  And doesn't need people at all.

When they heard the steel giant was to leave them
  The people of Mudfog went off it,
'But we made you!' they said, 'you can't leave us for dead,
  Just because you're not making a profit.'

But the steel giant could not be persuaded,
  'I no longer need you,' he scoffed,
'I'm leaving you here, and I'm off to Korea!'
  Then he upped and he went and he offed.

All children know giants are monsters
  Who travel in seven-league boots,
So don't be reliant on a corporate giant
  And small men in oversize suits.

All fairy-tales must have a moral,
     And this one is not rocket-science -
Control of the means of production's
     The best way to stand up to giants.

Andy Cro

Plastered in Port Clarence

It all starts with a mug of strong tea – no sugar thanks
and a chocolate digestive - doesn't matter where the crumbs fall.
The hot liquid hits the spot, lips dried with the back of his hand
then comes the politics.
'Fancy selecting Dobbo for Lord Mayor,
 wouldn't book him to run the bingo down the club.'
Probably the most essential tool of Sid's trade – his opinion.

That off his chest he scans the job
lost in his Michelangelo world
quiet eyes trained in dark corners
watched by his master
before entry into the Guild.
Alabaster fingers pick and smooth
sweep in a balletic pose.
Lays a cheek on the cold surface
squints and with a nod says 'Right.'

He presses clenched fists in the arch of his back
reaches down into the mouth of a friendly Puma
welcomed in castles and council flats
offered the best seat in the house 'just put it anywhere'
especially when it arrives on time as the man promised.

Inside the bag wood and metal compatible
angle trowels, floats, clean edges, polished handles
oblong pointed joint rules 'not often used now'.
There are large tools, small tools, lath hammer, hand board
crinkled tube of uni-bond – brushes with bristles
gauze trim, scrim cloth, countersunk nails
posi-drive, overdrive, wrist balm, tee-shirt
peaked cap for ceilings.

Red packet, board finish, green packet, mortar finish
whisked into double cream in a galvanized baby bath
scooped up, edged off, flicked on spread out
skimmed off, wet down, dried out then primed
and back, turn around, wide smile and a wink
thumbs up, sweep up, tools cleaned, paid up.
It all ends with a mug of strong tea – no sugar thanks
and a chocolate digestive – mind where the crumbs fall.

Monica Sharp

Mudfog Goes Bananas

The ballot boxes are all in,
  The crowds are going ape,
As in a photo-finish count
  The winner breasts the tape,

Then thumps his breast in victory
  To claim this late-night thriller,
For Mudfog's voted for a Mayor
  Resembling a gorilla.

Although it may seem comical
  To London media folk,
To citizens of Mudfog town
  Our leadership's no joke.

He may look like a chimpanzee,
  He may act like a fool,
He may sound like some nightmare
  Dreamed up by Pierre Boulle,

But it's not his fault if he's dumb,
  He can't help being a chimp,
According to the jungle law
  At least he's not a wimp.

In fact he is a primitive
Just like Jean-Jacques Rousseau's,
A noble savage standing tall,
  With hair between his toes.

He may be stupid, but he's ours,
  And not some Millbank flunkey.
If he's got fleas, he's proud of them:
  A proper Mudfog monkey.

Though some say it's embarrassing
  When voters break the mould,
That people shouldn't vote unless
  They vote the way they're told,

There's something in a simian
  That puts us at our ease,
Reminds us that it's not that long
  Since we were climbing trees,

That after all we're relatives,
  We share the DNA,
From King Kong down to Dubya
  These brutes are here to stay.

And there are those who argue that
  The voters were perplexed,
Because it's sometimes hard to tell
  One monkey from the next.

While Labour apes the Tories
  The day will come around
When folk will vote for those who drag
  Their knuckles on the ground.

There's some say that our critics
  Have got a bloody nerve,
That voters only ever get
  The leaders they deserve;

Democracy's a funny thing,
  They only want your vote
you vote for the monkey with
  Their rosette at its throat.

Meanwhile there are Psephologists
  And Darwinists who think
The Mayor of Mudfog may turn out
  To be the Missing Link,

The proof that progress can be stopped
  And put into reverse,
And that though things are pretty bad
  They'll keep on getting worse.

Banana-skin republics work
  Like any human zoo,
you throw people peanuts they'll
  Make monkeys out of you.

The final joke on which to choke,
  A pretzel-shaped reminder:
We may know who the monkeys are,
  But who's the organ grinder?

Andy Croft

Election Night in Mudfog

If you believe the ancient Chinese curse
  That interesting times are always grim,
Election nights put curses in reverse -
  The chances of excitement here are slim.

No issues here to set the world alight,
  The parties stretch from average to medium,
As though they really try with all their might
  To send us all to sleep with hype and tedium.

The more they claim that this election's vital,
  The less that anybody gives a toss
Which intellectual light-weight wins the title,
  And victory's just another name for loss.

The more they try to feed us fibs and lies,
  The more they try their best to reassure us,
The more we sleep because - surprise, surprise -
  Elections nights in Mudfog simply bore us.

Who cares about their futile panto capers
  When you could be tucked up asleep in bed?
When you can wait until the morning papers
  To learn that Mudfog politics is dead.

So if you still believe that Chinese curse,
  If interesting times still make you panic,
Remember that things always could get worse,
  You could be fast asleep on the Titanic.

Andy Crc

Cu chulaind's Lullaby
(on double time, cash in hand)

Snort, burlesque bull-bouncer
ow on Exchange Square,
canning herds in wattage orange

he valley's folded Christmas zeal
ours Nativity scenes from garage mouths

ll the streets, gritted roads
rittle avenues n' frosted groves
ght n' race for grottodom
o be the first He'll visit

h promise yeh

/ithout a doubt, the doormen tap-dance
ly with segs, slide n' shuffle, soak up stares
ke buffalo mounds in freezing fog

ulking shadows, black on grey
round megaliths, worn tumuli
nee-high bollards n' thin black ice

art n' bother clinging tight
opping slurred snogs n' covert gropes
nderneath the Green Man's bleep

arly doors

e queues are safe in the crack
a 22 carat tooth, ironed out
y a bleached blonde stare

x pupils swimming in each eye
x irises like jade tigers dancing the jitter
Redbull, tuned-in to the overflow
mood n' booze n' powdered highs

ys yeh then nah, in green, in red
ods 'em in then holds 'em back

no fuss
this hound will smile polite
to suss the yabber
even take a pinch of raw faced cheek

he cooks his paws
in white vinegar n' herbs, trained 'em
to kill with a simple tap

his bark has become rose quartz
spends the days carving edges
marking points in shifting maps

last orders

waits like a nail bomb for some tanked
-up bloke who's out to prove
a bitter point n' knows a few good moves

the hound is wired n' licensed to warp
the night back into shape, diffuse
the situation with a raised full glove

n' lead with his nut in a cold tamed rage
to gore with receded horns n' guard
the rites of Yuletide's turn

in dark dawn

after a parmo, a sleet squall drives
Cu chulaind home, inch by inch
he scrubs the night scents from his pours

before sneaking-in
between warm sheets to spoon
his body about Nemhain's sleep.

Bob Beagr

Long Lines At Skinningrove

A woman was brought up to bait the lines.
Sister, daughter, mother, wife,
had mussels to find for the coble's lines,
long, thousands-of-hooksworth lines.

Each hook needed a mussel
fetched up at low tide by a woman dressed
in a thick padded skirt, unstylishly short
to clear the slutch and clutching a doughnut
to fit on her head to carry a basketful.

A woman had to come up from Scarborough
and Whitby when their own musseld ran out
on account of the trawlers scouring the seabed.
They called it tilling and like the ploughing
that keeps the land fertile, but the small fry
and spawn, as well as the mussels, were gone
from the rocks and only limpets were left.

A woman called them flithers
and picking the flithers
was worse than gathering.
A woman would flit like a rook with her sisters
prising the suckers off with a knife
and when it came to the skaning they took longer
to scoop.

A woman's worst day was when the weather
was too bad for launching and the lines ready baited
lay in cobles for days turning rotten and slimy.
Bucking the lines was all work for nothing
and cobles laid up did not feed the children.

The trawling with nets sent the price of the catch
down to rock bottom and more longlines to bait
and a woman was glad
when a man left the fishing
and went down the mine.

Pat Brown

Salt

Sharp as Port Clarence salt,
part of a chemical reaction
too hot to halt,
they form and reform.

Rock deposits in the Tees bed,
they season the Valley with halite feats;
and, like Lot's wife, turn their heads
to look back at women of coal and steel
who've dissolved and become encrustations;
the 'salt licks' that feed us all.

In their new age, ice-like lustre,
who'd know that their mothers -
and their mothers' mothers -
were the salt-cakes of exchange,
the salaria on which tracks were laid,
chimneys smoked,
stacks flared.

Who'd know,
just looking at them,
shimmering like crystals -
that soon they'll be the brine
we're all surfing on.

Maureen Almo

Portrack Amazons

Moon women on the old curve of the Tees
settle for being mother and father
Artemis and Apollo in one.
They seek temporary union;
shield in The Willows,
tongues rattling like arrows in a quiver
planning the next chase;
and when torrents of children tumble
through the narrow gorges of the estate
gigantic loves are exiled, to stumble
between the borders of Swainby and Tilery.

The Beautiful Ones have no need of jewellery,
give them short skirts and hunting boots.

Maureen Almond

Muriel's Shop

Muriel lives in Hartlepool.
Muriel has a shop.
Her shop sells sandals
Stylish sandals
Eye-catching colourful
Stub toed round toed
Thong between toes
High heels wedge heels
No heel flip flops
Big toe captured
In soft leather loop.
Crocodile skin or beaded
Studded or embroidered
Soft chamois leather
Minimalistic thong.
Sandals to look pretty in
Not for walking
But to lounge on sunbed
In the noonday sun.
Sandals to tan your feet in
As well as the rest of you.
Not caring for feet
That should last a lifetime.
Saying BUGGER to the bunions.

Keith Porr

This Must Be It

swept through such storms towards him
spray-dazzled at eighty not stopping,
hollow with longing and sick,
to drive blind into a city shrouded in panic
until the phone breaks through,
his voice talking me in:
is there a fire station? go left; a bridge? cross it; straight on.
then the river, long cliffs of buildings, and a house,
a door standing in defiance of weather open.

To be given only what's needed:
a kettle boiled for strengthening tea,
toast buttered, with honey, tray softly placed;
a cover tucked round me, eyes closed, motionless, here.

To wake hearing him say: Mystery
that you are real on this sofa,
not a voice in the ansaphone.
As I notice the cover
(brave fuschia, her colour) stroking it,
what does he think?
he doesn't say.
The winter jasmine she put there alive
is fossilised tissuepaper-white and stands like halberds ready.)
moths brush antennae, knowing the dark,
under only at the approach of light.
He opens my present, Dunn's *Elegies*, - 'Not Donne's?' he says;
we share, fingertips touching, *Leaving Dundee.*

october evening soft as new bread;
we walk entwined along the harbourside, to candle light
eat, fingers salted with chips from one bowl,
tongues ravished spoon by spoon with passionfruit,
hearing St. Mary Redcliffe's bells at the wind's whim stop
then sound, as the great glazed door unlatching swings.

*And I think of my golden abutilon
re-flowering in the warm glass room
each calyx a brimstone butterfly
veined, fragile, radiant.*

Jo Heather

Architecture Avalanche

let's 'tend that you love me
        like I love you
and let's 'tend that I'm as beautiful as you.
    and just for one moment
    let's 'tend that we're together
    holding on to each other
            as much as each other pretends.

and let's 'tend that the world around us not collapsing
and let's 'tend that we are archways protecting each other
            from the falling rubble
                and the jumble
                and the trouble
                of all the architects around us
                that are making it double
            and the buildings and the houses
            and the bridges and the mumble
that are trying to tunnel their way inbetween.
they are chipping off bricks, one piece at a time.
but there is no mistake,
            and we cannot turn back,
so don't fear the avalanche anymore.

one rock at a time it comes tumbling down
    trying to break in, trying to beat us to the ground.
    but it won't go away, and it just won't work,
    'cause all you have to do is open your shirt
    and accept all those rocks in their colourful disguise
    because maybe one day you will just realise
    that the right and the wrong
    and the good and the bad
    and the stupid and the evil
    and the happy and the glad
            are o.k.

Claire Wa

94

While You Were Out

While you were out…
I've travelled through time,
all the way to Jane Mansfield & back.
Hoovering your workshop in a full circle dress,
 petticoats so stiff they stand up alone,
I've discovered the possibilities of domestic appliances.

While you were out…
I realized you're right, as far as you're concerned,
I never dress up anymore.
I save my glad rags for the dusting,
apply glamour where I need it the most,
before sniffing your scattered shorts so I can do the washing.

While you were out…
This sagging chest is wired into points
that could have the eyes out of the man in the moon.
I've drawn the line in a pencil skirt,
swollen to unfeasible dimensions.
I've been one of those women
who looks too good to speak.
One of those women with bolster arms,
 silk scatter-cushion lips men sink right into,
until I'm so deflated I can only sigh.

While you were out…
my skin has been stuffed tight
with honey, sugar, doll face.
I've burst at the re-enforced seams.
This hair has been short,
curled in milk licks around fingers,
trembling, fat as a pet lip.

And no, I did not ring the council.
I found my virginity down the back of the couch.
Lost it again by the time you got home.
I've been my own skin flick,
wished on by every star.

I bought the world. I sold the iron.
I layed the table.
And, yes, I cooked your dinner,
walked the dog. While you were out.

Angela Readman

Wash'n'Go

The first outward sign
Was that he stopped washing his hair,
An unwelcome eccentricity
In an otherwise personable man;
It was not the beginning,
But it was the first indicator.

Beneath the hair,
With its thickening crust,
Tectonic substrates
Were already uncoupling,
Titanic shelves and trenches
Had begun to unhinge,
To diverge or to overlap,
Crumbling at the edges,
Rumbling below the pitch of hearing,
Implacably re-aligning,
Until, eventually,
A new Antarctica was formed.

Initially, its vast iciness
Blocked all channels,
Prevented communication:
He was numbed
By the legion of fresh, blue-white choices.

Little flickers on the surface,
Like the hair,
Domestic infelicities,
And the occasional strange recipe –
Stir-fried bhajis
Being a particular unsuccess –
Were the only signals recorded;
But then
The recast geology,
The newer, colder framework
Underpinning his scalp,
Made itself evident,
Got a message through –

'I don't love you anymore,' he said,
Reaching for the shampoo.

Rowena Sommervi

My Nice Friend Hasn't Made Her Mind Up Yet

The grid of streets, the lines of orange lights –
Some nights I can hardly bear to look down.
I think of all the things that can go wrong,
Washing machines, cars, families….
World was in a mess when I got here.
No word, still. I'll throw rocks through her windows.
I sulk along the brow of the hill.
Strangers worm their way around my skull.
We think things that don't turn out to be right.
As if love will just fall out of the sky.
Some things I want to keep quiet about.
Are we disheartened? Never say never.
But I think it would have happened by now –
I mean, if it was going to happen.

John Harrison

Amoral

It's all been took, there's nothing left to take.
She's sweeping shattered glass to shattered piles,
her crunching footsteps amplify this ache.
It's all been took, there's nothing left to take.
Her life's been trashed, for someone's thirst to slake
and now replete the bastard sits and smiles.
It's all been took, there's nothing left to take,
she's sweeping shattered glass to shattered piles.

Gary Mir

Cutting a Tape in the Hostel

A man from the Congo, as wistful as a child
laments in a language that has no written words
gliding out the open window of the hostel;
a love song from a country at war. You've left
behind all those you care for. Don't think too much
out dub in flute and saxophone, a touch
of djembai with the wingbeat of migrating bird
and the breath of your guitar, a riff of surf
on shale, washing underneath the singer's slide.
Fold magic pennants in a pocket handkerchief
and scatter colour in grey faces where fear
has eaten into soul; what use is bitterness
in a cold welcome? Your wizardry will conjure
rhythm till the angels dance as if possessed.

Pauline Plummer

Note: *a djembai is an African drum*

The Car Gods

I have angered the car gods
And they will not be mocked.

I have not maintained my bodywork
I have not waxed and buffed
I have not sealed my rust
I have not scraped the bug stuff off the windscreen
I have not checked my levels
I have not added antifreeze
I have not hoovered up the bits of crisp.

I have taken my garage-man for granted
And complained at his bills
I have coveted my neighbour's whatever it is,
Simultaneously sneering.

I have driven whilst eating *and* changing tapes
I have skidded recklessly on loose chippings
I have been heedless on temporary road surfaces
And careless of the lack of road markings
I have overtaken in the rain.

I have been impatient with learner drivers
I have cursed caravans
I have ill-wished boy racers
I have driven up the arses of
Old people, as they enjoy the view,
And discuss the arrangements in their sisters' bungalows.

Once, inadvertently,
I ran over a cat.

Now, my gears are
Slipping
My clutch is
Flabby
My big end is
Too big
My suspension is
Suspended.

I have angered the car gods –
And they will be avenged.

Rowena Sommervil

How I learned to sing

The day spins like a plate on a pole,
sunlight streaming down and around us,
carving shadows out of the beach.
A snag of mishaps has shaped mum's face
into a taut parody of itself.
We are sent to find crabs, in pools
where we have not seen a crab for years.
The sea is a vein in the estuary,
the tide coming in a race memory,
and stranded pools dot the sand
with water still so cold it cramps
our calves before we can fight.
Then my sister is suddenly dancing,
splashing towards me with her discovery,
a small pink starfish she waves
in my dumbstruck face.
Though she is smaller, I can't reach it,
she ducks and swerves away
like the memory of it now.
I can't reach her, mum and dad
are too far back to help, but
I want that starfish, want to run
my fingers over its serrations,
pop it in my pocket to frighten
my mum with as we wipe sand
from between our toes later.
I start to scream at my sister,
first words and then just noises,
and the gulls turn from pencil flicks
to real birds with real blood
rushing beneath sharp feathers,
claws asking my shirt whether
I will rip or be carried off,
and now my voice has gone soft
and crying for what I can't get
I feel my wings rise and set,
the gulls' craws and my own throat
harmonise as I pale and float
up and over the docile waves,
not worrying, or wanting to be saved,
looking down on the strip of beach
and the family I could not reach,
and singing *back back back*.

Mark Robinson

Not This

I want to go waterskiing and hear Thucydides
not listen to George W Bush and plod so slowly

I want to be in Florence again, drinking whiskey
and talking and smoking Nazionale all night
then running out at six up into the hills
when running was like flying and I was yelling joy,
big enough to eat the world. Those hills round Florence could've
        flipped
up over onto my shoulders, I would've borne them easy, I
        would've bounced them
safe as eggshells

I want to be the mother I want to be -
able to carry her still when she's hurt, or worn right out,
spilling her my stories like sherbet, giving her everything I've
        loved
spending the bus fare home on chips and swinging back
        singing

I don't want to be wheeled around
I want to be back in Tottenham taking
a hat trick of wicked boys' wickets
gobsmacked they were, and I was perfect
my long arm and the ball and my brain and the stumps and the
        laws of Physics

back alone with my shadow on snow climbing Carrauntoohil
after a night drinking poteen in the hostel warden's friend's bac
        kitchen

I don't want to be this
the mad woman, bag woman, in tears on her knees down town
taking three goes to crawl into a taxi

I want that summer night in Dover Harbour Board's IT suite bac
writing a thousand lines of bugless code straight off
my brain and fingers tapdancing it out like Fred & Ginger
with the white cliffs applauding through the indigo
and Matthew Arnold's ghost singing along with me till daylight
when the whole thing runs clear first time

ot this hopeless fumbling to punch in a phone number, to
         sequence making toast

want to be reckless and generous
ot doling out steps,
ot schooling each day to the discipline of breath
ot counting my blessings, counting the birds that cut over my
         window,
ot learning patience

don't want to be this pale grey woman lying
aggered by the shapes of roofs
rilled by the colours the sky changes through
inging onto tapes of Seamus Heaney
:e a baby on a breast
icking the virtue out of his voice
acking the marrow out of his words
nable to read a word or write a word or find a word to say

want to be back reading Dostoyevsky like eating rum icecream
orging it, drunk on it, guzzling it, wild with it; back
rawled under the stars, stunned by them,
nning up Snowdon just after they faded

ot punching the walls too weakly to smudge the paper and
         crying through thin lungs
ot this not this not this please not this."

Liz Geraghty

The Exile

And though I love this land
As if it were my own,
A deeper knowing says it is not mine:
I cannot sense it in the bone
Or feel my feet welded to its earth
Like they do.
I have another home.

I cannot be
Apparent-careless of its beauty,
Accept it wordlessly
Like they do.
Mine is always the effusive thanks
Of a stranger being taken in.

Geoff Strang

My land my love, sleep well.
(Denis Brutus)

Two in the morning
helicopter lights strafe the yards
and gardens for twockers and burglars
a fight, a rape, a domestic.

Fog horns where the Tees
gapes at the sea.
Night shift sirens, goods trains, the all clear.
Sodium lights on the civic parks
Markers within the regiments of tulips
and conscripted daffodils.

Once thousands built titanic vats of molten flames
cooling towers.
Sweat, muscle, precision, injury;
Beer down the gullet
an ocean of coolness
to quench the fire of steel
but work shifts where men are more disposable.

Lads muscled from football and weights
exchange obscenities and spliffs
in alleys
tiny packs of heroin
in aluminium foil
like ancient coins,
dented, worn, creased.
quick brain shifts from logarithms
and cubic feet
calculating the millimetres between
the rubber sealing round a window frame
and the glass, to slide a sharp, thin
piece of steel towards the lock button,
easing it up.

Their bruised girls cockroach
the tunnel streets
moving on tall square heels;
they stand in one shoulder tops
numbed arms cut by the wind off the North Sea,
kids who can compute a car's lineage,
make of suit,
to a price.
My land, my love, sleep well.

Pauline Plummer

The SMELTER poets

Michael Affleck was born in Middlesbrough in 1977 and writes: 'i am my words and my words will change, so then, will i. wasn't i born beneath a blistering boro sky? and hasn't my eye drowned in the pleasures of the world already?'

Maureen Almond was born in Co. Durham and lives in Yarm. She studied for her MA at Newcastle University. Her pamphlet *HOT* (1997) and her first full-length collection *Tailor Tacks* (1999) are published by Mudfog. Her latest collection is *Oyster Baby*, published by Biscuit (2002).

Katharine Banner lives and works on a dairy farm in North Yorkshire on a tributary of the River Tees. Her poems have been published in magazines and in pamphlet form and a collection entitled 'Aerial Photography' is due from Mudfog shortly.

Bazala Bashir is 25 years old and was born in Middlesbrough. She won the Middlesbrough Poet Laureate competition in 1999 and had a pamphlet of poems entitled 'No Small Fire' published by Mudfog the same year. She now lives, works and studies in France.

Bob Beagrie lives in Middlesbrough. Published in magazines, a pamphlet *Gothic Horror* (Mudfog 1995) and *Masque: The Art of the Vampyre* (2000). Won the 2003 Biscuit Poetry Prize resulting in a first collection, 'Huginn & Muninn', recently won a Time to Write Northern Writers Award.

Ian Brelstaff was born in the Tees Valley area, lives there, grows vegetables there, walks there, drives there, draws and paints there, has so many good friends there, and occasionally, very occasionally, writes about being there.

Pat Brown lives in Saltburn. Pat has been a solicitors' clerk, market researcher, Parish Councillor, teacher. Now retired to be a poet, member of Saltburn Writers' Group and Hall Garth Poets, a School Governor and a great grandma. Publications include *Raining is no excuse* (Mudfog).

... Chesterfield has lived and worked in the Tees Valley area for a number of years.

Carol Cooke was born in the north east, lived and worked here much of her life lecturing, with the BBC, now at the University of Teesside. Married, two sons, one granddaughter, Grace, who makes her very happy. Carol writes anything and everything, always returns to poetry.

Bob Cooper's won five pamphlet competitions in just over six years. Th[e] last pamphlet, *Pinocchio's Long Neb*, is still available from Smith Doorsto[p] and his full collection, *All We Know Is All We See*, is available fro[m] Arrowhead Press (http:www.arrowheadpress.co.uk). He lives in Nunthorp[e].

Andy Croft has written many books, including five books of poetr[y] *Nowhere Special, Gaps Between Hills, Headland, Just as Blue* and *Gre[at] North*. In 2000 he was Poet-in-Residence on the Great North Run and [is] currently Writer-in-Residence at HMP Holme House, Stockton.

Liz Geraghty was born in Staithes and grew up in Middlesbrough, whe[re] she lives now with her daughter.

John Harrison is a fifty-three year old factory worker from East Clevelar[d]. Mudfog published his *Not The Last Bus Back From Loftus* in 2001. He [is] keen on music and likes to practise the saxophone. His neighbours practi[se] patience.

Jo Heather moved to Teesside when she married in 1970 . She worked [as] a social worker in mental health until retiring to live and write on the ed[ge] of the North Yorks. moors. She has three grown up children.

Shirley Hetherington: born and raised in Middlesbrough. An ex-jun[ior] teacher who has had poetry published in anthologies and a Mudf[og] collection, *Shiny Days*. Her children's book *The Voyage of the Ark*, w[ith] illustrations by her daughter , is currently being prepared for publication[.]

Mollie Hill was raised in Middlesbrough, spent most of her working life [in] the NHS. She gained her degree through the O.U. and continued creati[ve] writing studies with Leeds University. Her *Seed Corn* sequence w[as] published in *Throughroutes* (with Ann O'Neill and Molly Maughan, Mudf[og] 1999)

Norah Hill teaches creative writing to people with disabiliti[es]. Middlesbrough Poet Laureate 2001-2, Norah has published two poe[try] collections and a book of stories. Her work has appeared in *Stand* and [*...] *Review*. She is currently writing poetry based on the Book of Psalms.

Anne Hine has lived and worked in the north for 30 years. She lives a[nd] writes in Stockton and is a member of Vane Women, a writing, perform[ing] and publishing group. Her first pamphlet *Dark Matters* was published [in] 2001.

Gordon Hodgeon now works part-time and is involved in several local writing initiatives including Mudfog Press. Last book was *A Cold Spell* (Mudfog, 1996, out of print). Poems published recently in *The Penniless Press, Red Sky At Night* (Five Leaves, 2003), *Biscuit 2003 Anthology*.

Marilyn Longstaff is a member of Vane Women. Poems published in magazines e.g. *Tears in the Fence, Fire, Mslexia* and *Smiths Knoll*. First pamphlet *Puritan Games* published by Vane Women Press (2001). Marilyn received a 2003 Northern Promise Award towards developing a full-length collection.

Val Magee is a Middlesbrough performance poet. She has performed at arts and comedy venues around the North East and has facilitated literature and arts projects across Teesside.

Gary Ming is a 38 year old native of Middlesbrough, ex-bricklayer, ex-steel erector, ex-junkie who was introduced to poetry by Andy Croft while in prison. Mudfog is publishing Gary's work in a separate pamphlet in the autumn of 2003.

Brian Morton lives with his wife, Denise, and six dogs in Redcar. He began work as an industrial chemist with Dorman Long (British Steel) in 1961 and has been writing for over twenty years. He is currently Chairman of Redcar Writers.

Jan O'Neill started writing in 1990. She had a pamphlet *Quicksteps* published by Mudfog in1994 and has had work included in anthologies: *Breathless* ,1994, *A Hole Like That* (Scratch1994) and *Throughroutes* (with Polly Maughan and Mollie Hill, Mudfog 1999).

Pauline Plummer, once of Liverpool, has published widely. 3 poetry collections, including *Demon Straightening* (Iron 2000). Awarded the Tyrone Guthrie Poetry and Ignite Awards. Teaches creative writing at Northumbria University, has worked in schools, prisons and adult ed. in the UK and Africa.

Keith Porritt was born in 1935, left school at 14, started work at Cargo Fleet Steelworks as a messenger boy and moved on to design engineer in aerospace and nuclear power, before becoming a teacher. Keith has been writing poetry since his retirement.

Angela Readman was born and grew up in Middlesbrough. She moved to Newcastle to do her MA and stayed. Angela writes poetry and prose. Her first poetry collection, *Colours/Colors*, was published by Diamond Twig (2001). Iron Press featured her work in a trilogy of female poets *Unholy City* (2002).

Mark Robinson was born in Preston, Lancs., lives in Preston-on-Tees. Edit[c] of SCRATCH magazine and press, he's done various things in the arts in th[e] Tees Valley. Now Director of Arts and Development at Arts Council Englan[d] NE. Books include *Half A Mind* and *The Horse Burning Park*.

Monica Sharp was born and raised in Port Clarence. She welcomes th[e] opportunity to write for SMELTER. Her work has been published by Mudf[c] and appeared in various anthologies including *Ek Zuban*, a cross-cultur[al] collaboration of literary traditions in the Tees Valley.

Rowena Sommerville has worked as a children's writer and illustrator (thr[ee] books published) and as a textile artist. She currently manages a variety [of] arts projects across Teesside. She sings in and writes material for th[e] acappella band *Henwen*. **Geoff Strange** was born in Bristol and came [to] Teesside in 1978 to take up a lecturing post. He never left. Now retired, [h]e started writing five years ago as he no longer had any excuses not to. It [is,] Geoff says, a great adventure.

Claire Ward lives near Whitby and is currently part way through a one ye[ar] M.A. Fine Art course in Sunderland University. She takes photos of hers[elf] in theatrical looking costumes, then uses these and her writing to crea[te] relief montage images.

Ruth Ward was born in Linlithgow and specialised in Theatre Nursi[ng] following her training in Edinburgh. Eighteen years ago she came to live [in] Middlesbrough. Ruth enjoys walking on the moors and is interested [in] wildlife and the environment.

Andy Willoughby comes from Eston. He attended Kent University where [he] achieved a First in Literature and the University's T.S. Eliot Prize. He runs *T[he] Hydrogen Jukebox Cabaret of the Spoken Word* in Darlington and [was] Middlesbrough Poet Laureate 2002-3.

Other current MUDFOG titles

Katharine Banner:	**Aerial Photography**	£6.00
Norman Cowell:	**Big Mag**	£4.00
May Gill:	**Dear Bob**–Letters from Home 1930-31	£5.99
Norah Hill:	**Like** (Middlesbrough Poet poems, 2002)	£3.50
Marion Husband:	**Service**	£3.00
Gary Ming:	**Give It a Try**	£3.00
Maureen Almond:	**Tailor Tacks**	£5.95
John Miles Longden:	**LP's and Singles**	£5.95

All titles are available from:

Independent
Northern
Publishers

The Independent Northern Publishers
P.O Box 990, Newcastle upon Tyne, NE99 2US.

Tel: 0191 212 0354 / 07956 402 408

www.**northernpublishers**.co.uk

Email: **crista**@zoom.co.uk